EMANCIPATION
HELL

THE TRAGEDY WROUGHT

BY

LINCOLN'S

EMANCIPATION PROCLAMATION

KIRKPATRICK SALE

Produced in the Republic of South Carolina by

SHOTWELL PUBLISHING LLC
Post Office Box 2592
Columbia, So. Carolina 29202

WWW.SHOTWELLPUBLISHING.COM

Cover Design based on "Emancipation Proclamation," Lithograph. (J.S. Smith & Company, 1890) and executed by Boo Jackson Graphics.

This edition is an AUTHORIZED REISSUE of the author's 2012 self-published work *Emancipation Hell: The Tragedy Wrought by Lincoln's Emancipation Proclamation. 150 Years Ago.*

PUBLISHER'S NOTE

WE WOULD LIKE to publicly thank and personally acknowledge the generosity of the author, Kirkpatrick Sale, for allowing us to repackage, reformat, and reissue this important, timely, and iconoclastic work.

TABLE OF CONTENTS

"As affairs have turned, it is the central act of my administration, and the great event of the nineteenth century."

— Abraham Lincoln to Francis Carpenter, 1864

"An annihilation of individual property rights without parallel in the history of the modern world."

— R. R. Palmer, A History of the Modern World, 1950

I. Emancipation Hell, 1862

THE SUMMER OF 1862 was particularly hot in Washington, D.C., and Abraham Lincoln spent as little time in the stuffy White House as he could, preferring to spend his evenings at the cottage at the Soldiers' Home a few blocks to the north. But on Tuesday, July 22, he ordered a special meeting of his seven-man cabinet there, in the oval library on the second floor instead of his own office on the first, an indication that he felt a little sense of ceremony was appropriate.

"I said to the cabinet," Lincoln recalled later, "that I had resolved upon this step, and had not called them together to ask their advice, but to lay the subject-matter of a proclamation before them." A proclamation, he said, on "the adoption of the emancipation policy." Emancipation. Finally, it seemed, the President was taking the bold step that so many radicals in his party and most of the abolitionists throughout the North had been urging upon him for the better part of the last year, his first in office.

The reaction was a careful silence. "Little was said," remembered Gideon Welles, the Navy Secretary, "by any one but the President." He proceeded to read from two sheets of lined vellum on which he

1

had written in his small, careful hand a sort of legal document, two pages long, with none of the grandeur and elegance he would evince in other statements. It was, he asserted, a "war measure," taken under his authority as Commander-in-Chief, and had no need to acquire Congressional assent. After all, if he had used his war powers to bypass Congress to suspend habeas corpus, as he did in April 1861, to arrest and imprison perhaps 15,000 Northern critics without trial, to shut down more than 300 newspapers for varying periods, to censor telegraph communication, to issue postal censorship, to create a naval blockade of the South, to declare martial law in Delaware, and to invade Maryland and rig elections there to keep it from seceding — and, as a matter of fact, to declare war without Congressional authorization — then why should this be any more problematic?

The first paragraph was a dry assent to a bill Congress had passed a few days earlier allowing confiscation of property of those "participating in, aiding, countenancing, or abetting the existing rebellion...as within and by said sixth section provided." Nothing here, they must have thought — this couldn't be why a special cabinet session was called. The second paragraph turned to a scheme Lincoln had advanced before, getting Congress to pass a law giving Federal aid to any Southern states that would recognize the Union and voluntarily adopt the "gradual abolishment of slavery," a measure to restore the Union, the reason that "the war, as it has been, will be, prosecuted." Nothing here, either — every man there had heard this idea and knew it had scant support in the legislature.

But then Lincoln turned the page and announced, "And, as a fit and necessary military measure for effecting this object, I...do order and declare that on the first day of January in the year of Our Lord one thousand, eight hundred and sixty-three, all persons held as slaves within any state or states" in rebellion from the United States "shall then, thenceforward, and forever, be free."

The logic was not precisely clear — it did not seem that the abolition of slavery in seceding states would necessarily promote the cause of union — but this was indeed something new for the Federal government: a declaration that it had the power to rescind the laws of states in secession because it was fighting a war against them, and that in wartime the confiscation, or liberation, of the enemy's property could be held to be legitimate. A modern nationalistic state was taking shape, one absorbing power from the states into its center, and willing to declare and fight a war to achieve it.

Mark you, the declaration did not apply to the states *not* in rebellion where slavery flourished (Maryland, Delaware, Kentucky, and Missouri) because at its heart its intent was not so much to create free people as to foster slave rebellions in the South (especially on plantations whose owners had gone to war) and to disrupt the food production on which the Confederate army depended. (Lincoln the politician also had no desire to alienate slave-owners in the Border States who were, after all, men whose votes he would need at the next election.) In other words, as Secretary of State William Seward remarked ironically at the time,

> We show our sympathy with slavery by emancipating
> slaves where we cannot reach them and holding them
> in bondage where we can set them free.

Nonetheless, the cabinet members were receptive to the proclamation, with only a few demurs. Attorney General Edward Bates argued that it had to go hand in hand with compulsory colonization, a resettlement of freed slaves to South America or Africa, an idea that Lincoln had previously championed but without support from a Congress that feared the cost; Treasury Secretary Salmon Chase worried that its sweeping power to annul state laws would not be upheld by Federal courts, a fear that Lincoln had earlier expressed, and that "universal emancipation" would set off "depredation and massacre" across the South; Seward said that it seemed like "the last measure of an exhausted government" and

3

should not be issued until some signs of Union success on the battlefield, lest the public regard it as without any effect, as, he pointed out, the famous papal bull against Halley's comet.

Lincoln heard their responses but was not inclined to engage in a long discussion. He had come to announce his decision, not to ask for advice. In fact he was inclined to issue the proclamation the next day, and only a fervent plea by Seward at a meeting that evening persuaded him to delay. But only for the opportune moment, the right Union success, and he figured that would not be long. For this was something that, as a "military measure," he was determined to do when the time was right.

Lincoln grew impatient enough after waiting two months to decide to regard the clash between General George McClellan and the Confederacy's General Robert Lee at Sharpsburg, Maryland—when Lee was forced to retreat across the Potomac on September 17 after a full day of battle—as a Union victory. True, Lee's Army of Northern Virginia was driven out of Maryland into Virginia, and it did suffer immense casualties of over 10,000 (perhaps 2,700 killed), including his wife Mary's half -brother, but McClellan didn't take the chance to cross the river and drive it back farther, and his troops had similar vast casualties of more than 12,000 (maybe 2,108 killed). Pretty much a standoff, and it is hard to see, with such awful slaughter as that — what would turn out to be the deadliest single day in the history of American warfare—how a reasonable man could regard that as a victory for anyone. Nonetheless, Lincoln chose to overlook this unprecedented immensity of bloodshed, foreshadowing a war of unprecedented gore, and proclaimed the Sharpsburg standoff a Union triumph.

So on the Sunday, four days after the battle, Lincoln holed himself up in the White House, rewriting the proclamation, with the idea that he would publish this form immediately to alert the country of his intentions, then make the formal proclamation on January 1 of the coming year, when it would go into effect. On the following day at the regular meeting of the cabinet, he sprang it on them.

This time they knew what was coming, but there may have been some surprise in Lincoln's remarks in introducing it. "When the rebel army was at Frederick," he told them, as Salmon Chase would later remember, "I determined, as soon as it should be driven out of Maryland, to issue a Proclamation of Emancipation such as I thought likely to be useful. I said nothing to anyone, but I made the promise to myself, and — to my maker." Maker? Lincoln, who was not a particularly religious man, and in his youth had in fact been a proclaimed skeptic, had never before brought God into his politics, nor dared to aver that he came to decisions by making pledges to the heavens, a position that he knew would probably discomfit his hard-headed cabinet colleagues. "This might seem strange," Lincoln admitted, but "God had decided this question in favor of the slaves." It is as if he now wanted to have a prodigious ally for this eventful step and, indeed, one with whom to share the blame should it not turn out well.

Lincoln then started to read from the four sheets of paper on which he had written the proclamation, now become a straight-out military pronouncement. He began with the previous paragraph that the war was being fought for "restoring the constitutional relation" between the Union and the rebellious states and where that was restored he would have Congress offer aid to the states that would "voluntarily adopt" immediate or gradual "abolishment of slavery." He then restated the emancipation paragraph of the document of July — all slaves in the seceding states "shall be then, thenceforward, and forever free" as of January 1 — but added, so that there could be no comparison to papal bulls, that the full military might of the Union would be used to "recognize [later, at Seward's suggestion, he added "and maintain"] the freedom of such persons" and do nothing to hinder "any efforts they may make for their actual freedom," including, it was implied, armed insurrection.

He then pulled out lengthy quotations from the articles of war act that Congress had passed in March, forbidding "all officers or persons in the military or naval service" from returning fugitive slaves, and the confiscation act passed in July that ordered slaves escaping to the Union armies would be deemed "captives of war, and shall be forever free." To ensure that the proclamation would be seen as within the legitimate province of a commander-in-chief he added that he ordered "all persons engaged in the military and naval service of the United States to observe, obey, and enforce" the acts he cited.

It was a document of some tediousness, despite the subject at its core, and the cabinet had heard most of its language before, so after a "long and earnest" discussion raised no substantive objections. Postmaster General Montgomery Blair allowed as how he was afraid of what effect this would have on the border states, where slavery was unaffected, and the Army, whose men had not enlisted to become instigators of black rebellions, but he realized that Lincoln would not be deterred at this point. Far from it—the President gave the pages to Seward and ordered that it be issued as a State Department circular the next day, and had copies made for the Senate and House of Representatives. The War Department was ordered to issue 15,000 copies for distribution among the commanders and their troops.

In the following hundred days before the final proclamation would be officially issued on New Year's Day, the nation greeted the document with every emotion from alarm to zeal. A great many, mostly Republicans, and several important Republican newspapers, including Horace Greeley's *New York Tribune*, were able to see in it, despite deficiencies, the triumph of the abolitionists' dream, although in fact no free men would necessarily be created by it and the chance of its having an effect in the Confederacy was, at least at this point, minimal. Others saw it as likely to seriously damage Republican chances at the polls in the midterm elections coming up in October and November, since Northern citizens in general were apprehensive about hordes of freed slaves coming into their states to settle, and Democrats would make the most of it. A number of lawyers challenged the document's legality, and one Republican Congressman offered as "my judgment as a lawyer" that since it was just a presidential decree "in point of law, no court will hold it a valid title to freedom" — a point that Lincoln himself, also a lawyer, was forced to agree with, but he hoped it would have had its effect before any legal challenge was upheld. ("The original proclamation has no...legal justification," he once confessed to Secretary Chase)

The strongest sentiments, however, lay with those who opposed the proclamation as inflammatory and misguided. An interesting record of how these were received at the White House comes from one of Lincoln's faithful aides, William Stoddard: "How many editors and how many other penmen within these past few days rose in anger to remind Lincoln that this is a war for the Union only, and they never gave him any authority to run it as an Abolition war. They never, never told him that he might set the Negroes free, and, now that he has done so, or futilely pretended to do so, he is a more unconstitutional tyrant and a more odious dictator than ever he was before."

Even in the quarters where Lincoln might have anticipated a warm reception — the free black population of the North — the proclamation was greeted with some trepidation, at least by those who bothered to see what the document actually said, since it was very narrow in its impact and indeterminate as to its actual effect. Frederick Douglass for example, the black abolitionist who had urged the President to go all out with a provision for enlisting black troops to "raise the banner of Emancipation among the slaves," was disappointed in both its timidity and its tone, with not "one expression of sound moral feeling against Slavery, one word of regret and shame that this accursed system had remained so long." (Indeed, that Lincoln, a man capable of great eloquence, issued so flat and technical a document suggested that the actual evil of bondage played no part in his emancipation strategy.)

He did not mention it, but he must have noticed the absence of any reference to a policy of enlisting blacks, either from North or South, as soldiers in the Union army. That was an idea that had been bruited about for some time—Lincoln's first Secretary of War had issued a report urging that slaves should be emancipated and armed in 1861—but Lincoln resisted it, knowing that Union soldiers' racism went deep and such a move was likely to bring recruitment to a halt; he rescinded the order and fired the secretary. And when a general of his—David Hunter, in command of the Department of the South, in Port Royal, South Carolina—issued his own martial law and decree of emancipation in April and May of 1862, followed by enrolling 500 former slaves into a First South Carolina Volunteers unit, Lincoln immediately put a halt to it and reprimanded the general. Arming freed black slaves was a dangerous thing to do, and it would arouse Northern passions to fears of unchecked black insurrections and, as one Kentucky Congressman put it, a war of "murder, conflagration, and rapine."

And yet, Northern recruitment was now flagging, eighteen months into the war. Lincoln remarked in a letter on September 28, six days after the preliminary proclamation was issued, that "it was not very satisfactory" that since then "the stocks have declined, and troops come forward more slowly than ever." The war was still not going well, McClellan was still standing pat in Maryland, complaining of insufficient troops, and something clearly had to be done. Whether in secret or in consultation with some of his cabinet it is not clear, but by December the President decided to put forthright language into the final declaration that would authorize that freed slaves would be "received into the armed service of the United States." It was of course risky but it seemed a necessity, and people who had spent a lifetime in servitude ought to be malleable soldiers, and with special ardor to fight for the side that had brought about their emancipation.

As for Congress, sitting in a lame-duck session, it was so divided about the proclamation that it went back and forth in debate for a month without taking any action at all, denying Lincoln the public support he had asked for. The Republicans, in the majority, could have pushed through a resolution in favor of the proclamation, but the very limited nature of the document, applying only to Southern slaves and giving the Confederacy a hundred days to comply, as well as its offers of compensated emancipation to the border states and a Federal effort to colonize freed slaves, drew fire from the Radical Republicans, and the Democrats were unanimous in opposing the whole thing as, one said, "unconstitutional and shocking to the civilization of the age."

As the deadline drew near, Lincoln consulted two more times with his cabinet and made several modifications. Bates, Seward, and Chase urged him to cut the phrase after "the freedom of such persons" that promised the government would not repress "any efforts they may make for their actual freedom" as encouraging insurrectionary uprising and alarm those who feared it spreading to the North. Lincoln acquiesced and suggested that he add something about the freed slaves being urged to "abstain from all violence" and even "labor faithfully for reasonable wages," however unlikely that would come about—especially since the proclamation made no mention of compensation for the slave owners, who might then become employers, or of job training for the slaves, who might then earn reasonable wages. He then added a suggestion that they take out the word "forever" from the phrase "henceforward forever shall be free," since his lawyerly mind thought that this might be challenged in court as going beyond the limits of a proclamation valid only in time of war, and the rest agreed. Finally, Chase came forward with a closing sentence that managed to jumble together appeals to the Constitution, the Declaration, God, war, humankind, and justice: "Upon this act, sincerely believed to be an act of justice, warranted by the Constitution [which had in fact defended slavery], upon military

9

necessity, I invoke the considerate judgment of mankind, and the gracious favor of Almighty God." Lincoln liked it and in it went.

Then on December 1, one month before the proclamation would be issued, Lincoln included an extraordinary passage in his annual message to Congress. He proposed that Congress pass, and the state legislatures approve, a new constitutional amendment that provided for three elements of slave emancipation that were totally at odds with the January edict. First, it would authorize *gradual* emancipation by the slave states "at any point before 1900," as "way to spare both races from the evils of sudden derangement" and to spare freed blacks "from the vagrant destitution that must largely attend immediate emancipation." Second, it would provide that "any state, wherein slavery now exists...shall receive compensation" for the freed slaves financed by the Federal government for several generations. (As Lincoln knew, compensation had been used in emancipation throughout South America and in the British, French, and Danish colonies — and even in Washington itself in 1862.) Third, it would authorize Congress to appropriate money "for colonizing free colored persons...at any place or places outside of the United States."

This was so extraordinary because it did everything that the Proclamation a month later did not (the previous promise to colonize freed slaves was dropped in the final version), and it offered a plan of emancipation that well might have worked, or at any rate worked better by far than the absence of plan in the final document. It did not have the idea of immediate freedom that made the other so attractive to some, but it had a far more realistic and solid appreciation of the complexities in the process of true freedom. And had it been passed it would have had a far greater impact on the war, for it well might have attracted some Confederate states and it almost surely would have worked on the border slave states, providing a half a million black freed men for the army.

But it was too rational, too moderate for the Radical Republicans and abolitionists in and out of Congress, who in their ideological frenzy wanted a Proclamation whether or not it freed a single slave. Congress never even took it up.

On New Year's Day 1863, when the proclamation was issued, the Government Printing Office ran off a two-page broadsheet with, for the first time, the words "Emancipation Proclamation" across the top, and that evening a leaked copy was printed in the *Washington Evening Star* and sent out on the wires.

Henry Raymond, editor of the *New York Times,* printed the document the next day with an approving editorial that asserted that "President Lincoln's proclamation...marks an era, in the history, not only of this war, but of his country and the world." Lincoln himself took an even broader view: "It is the central act of my administration," he would say two years later, "and the great event of the nineteenth century."

And so indeed it was, but for reasons far beyond Lincoln's pretense that he had brought freedom to the black people of the South. For in fact he had not, as time was to show. What he had done was to set in motion a terrible chain of events that would lead to an increasingly savage campaign of war by the Northern army now endowed with a moral righteousness that permitted it to fight civilians as well as soldiers and pillage and burn and raze all in its path; to a military occupation of the South that brought freedom to no one and imposed a system of unjust Republican rule for eleven disastrous years; to a deliberate national policy of Southern subjugation after Union troops withdrew that brought impoverishment to vast swathes of both whites and blacks throughout the South; and by neglecting the fate and future of the former black slaves and turning the national back on the "Negro question," to the creation of racial disparity and enmity that would last with varying degrees of severity for the next hundred years or more.

Emancipation, yes: emancipation hell. We cannot understand the war and its full consequences, we cannot understand the history of race relations for the next one hundred and fifty years, including today, and we cannot understand the South and its position in the modern republic, unless we understand that.

II. TRANSFORMATION AND ESCALATION, 1863-1865

REACTION TO PUBLICATION of the final Emancipation Proclamation was predictable. Abolitionists and the Radical Republicans hailed it, of course, though it is not always clear if they had actually read it or were only in favor of the idea behind it. Typical was William Lloyd Garrison, a leading abolitionist, who wrote in his paper, *The Liberator*, that the document "was a great historic event, sublime in its magnitude, momentous and beneficent in its far-reaching consequences." Similarly, abolitionist Moncure Conway saw that "a victorious sun appeared about to rise upon the New World of free and equal men." And of course Frederick Douglass, though he was careful to spell out its motivations: "Common sense, the necessities of the war, to say nothing of the dictation of justice and humanity have at last prevailed. We shout for joy that we live to record this righteous decree."

And so did many other freed blacks in the North. That Sunday night and for several nights after prayer services were held in black churches in Boston, New York, Chicago, Philadelphia, and some other cities, and in a few places parades and parties generally called "jubilees." Even in Norfolk, Virginia, which had been specifically ruled out as having the Proclamation apply, several thousand blacks paraded while thousands more looked on. Blacks in the South were in large part kept ignorant of the Proclamation, though in several Union-controlled areas former slaves moved into army encampments or volunteered as soldiers (in Port Royal some even formed the First South Carolina Volunteers under the command of Colonel Thomas Higginson). More ominous was the practice in Federally occupied Corinth, Mississippi, where officers told the local slaves that they were free and issued them pistols in order to go to their masters and "act as missionaries" to liberate others.

But in a great many places in the North, speeches and commentaries and editorials not swept up in the fervor of the abolitionists were critical of the decree. New York Governor Horatio Seymour, who was elected as a critic of emancipation, called it a "bloody, barbarous, revolutionary, and unconstitutional scheme." The *Louisville Daily Democrat* sputtered: "We scarcely know how to express our indignation at this flagrant outrage of all constitutional law, all human justice, all Christian feeling." The *Harrisburg Patriot and Union* in Pennsylvania said that by having the Army do nothing "to repress rebellion" of blacks in the South was creating a "cold-blooded invitation to insurrection and butchery."

And even many who were in general support of the principle of the proclamation pointed out its major flaws—flaws in fact that Lincoln himself was keenly aware of and indeed had tried to correct in the proposal for a constitutional amendment he had just made to Congress.

To begin with, many questioned whether there was any Constitutional legitimacy for Lincoln's presumed war powers—nothing of the kind appears in the Constitution, only a provision for the President as "Commander-in-Chief"—or for him to nullify and repeal valid laws passed by the states. For him to assert a "power of emancipation" from his "power to make war," declared New Jersey Governor Joel Parker, a "War Democrat," was in effect to assert "a power to change Constitutional rights" at his personal pleasure. Besides, whatever war powers might exist, he added, they applied to soldiers and battlefields, not civilians over a stretch of eleven states, and trying to assert Presidential rule over people "who held slaves under the State laws" would be as valid as if the President were to "notify Queen Victoria...in what part of her Indian dominions the sepoys shall be emancipated."

Then many noted that the whole question of compensation, which Lincoln had been at such pains to elaborate in his Constitutional proposal to Congress, was entirely left out, much to the dismay also of several members of the Cabinet. If it was true, as Lincoln had said, that slavery was a national project, then its abolition was also national, and the Federal government had an obligation to pay the slave owners something for the property it was taking from them—and that would, moreover, make many more in the South, and the Border states as well, willing to cooperate. Lacking such a provision, the Proclamation could not possibly have any real effect in the South, except to arouse immediate opposition.

Also left out was the core question of what to do with former slaves if they managed to gain their freedom, particularly after the war if the Union was victorious, when there would be about 3.5 million people with no clear status and no provisions for economic or political integration into existing society. Lincoln's favorite solution was colonization—"restoring a captive people," as he once put it, "to their long-lost father-land, with bright prospects for the future" — but since he had made no headway with Congress on that score, he thought it best to keep it out of the Proclamation as being inappropriate in a strictly war measure. As to the question of an economic future for the freedmen, Lincoln rejected the idea of providing them with land of their own to farm on — usually expressed as "forty acres and a mule" — and instead thought in terms, as he wrote in a letter eight days after the Proclamation, of adopting "systems of apprenticeship for the colored people" and creating contractual agreements between whites and blacks "by which the two races could gradually live themselves out of their old relation to each other." Yet none of that was dealt with in the Proclamation either, which would prove to be a sure prescription for hostility between the races and penury for the large majority of freed blacks after the war.

Some have argued, Edgar Lee Masters in 1931 most persuasively, that the failure of the Proclamation, and the subsequent government, to address the issue of the economic future of the South and the freedmen's place in it was not an oversight but a deliberate strategy on behalf of the corporate and industrial interests in the Republican Party, in the heat of its Hamiltonianism, that intended to "plunder the South" after it was defeated. "Piety and plunder in the person of the new capitalist," Masters argued, "by the use of sectional hatred took over the control of Congress" and eventually used that power to send treasury agents into the South "looking for property to confiscate," particularly for Northern railroads, and, making "common cause with local thieves and stole everything they could find in the way of cotton, tobacco and corn." Certainly that seems to be what was in Lincoln's mind early on; as he told an Interior Department official in 1862, in the next year "the character of the war will be changed. It will be one of subjugation... The South is to be destroyed and replaced by new propositions and new ideas." And so it happened.

The proclamation was decidedly unpopular with the Union soldiers, whose general attitude was expressed by one officer who declared that "I do not want to fight for Lincoln's proclamation one day longer" and another who reported that his men were strongly against it, many of them "boldly stating that they would not have entered the army had they thought such would have been the action of the government." And Admiral Andrew Foote noted that it was having a "baneful" effect on the troops, "producing discontent at the idea of fighting only for the negro." The response all over was desertion—a Vermont soldier reported in January that "it is nothing uncommon for a Capt. to get up in the morning and find half his company gone"—and it is estimated that as many as 200,000 Union soldiers deserted around this time and eventually about 350,000, fully 16 per cent of the total force.

The mutiny that many had feared, including General-in-Chief Henry Hallek, did not occur, but the effect of the desertions on the army was serious enough that it pressured Congress to pass the first conscription act in March of that year. That proved extremely unpopular and it is thought that some 90,000 young men fled to Canada to escape the draft and perhaps that many simply took to the hills out of the range of the Army enrollment officers. A riot in New York City by men refusing to be drafted to free black men who might then compete with them for laboring jobs went on for a week, with black men being murdered and a black orphanage being set on fire. It had to be put down by five regiments of troops who mowed down several hundred men to restore order. Enough men eventually were drafted to get the army functioning again, but it was not until ex-slaves were accepted (and sometimes physically forced) into the Union ranks and trained—perhaps 100,000 in all, from 1863 to 1865, along with maybe 100,000 Northern blacks—that the force was up to its pre-Proclamation levels.

The treatment of blacks in Union service was only a slight improvement over their former lives. They were not given pay equal to white soldiers until June 1864, and when men of the Massachusetts regiments refused to fight without equal pay they were court-martialed and slain. Most men served as menial laborers, in forts and garrisons, and few were used in battle, and when they did face enemy fire, as did the 54th Massachusetts regiment in South Carolina, they were usually assigned the ugliest forays that were little more than suicidal. Congress ruled early in 1863 that blacks could not be field officers, so during the war fewer than a hundred held any rank above sergeant and those were mostly chaplains or medical personnel without commands. And wherever they were, black recruits faced unwavering racism from virtually all their white colleague. An observer for the New York City Union League in 1864 gave what seemed to be a general assessment of blacks in service when he said that the recruits of the 20th Regiment "were abused worse than any negroes had been on the plantations" by their white officers.

Those recruited into the service, however, paled in numbers to those who fled behind Northern lines and could not be made to serve—women, children, aged, and infirm—whom the army designated, for some reason, "contrabands." Since it had to accept these blacks who became effectively free only when coming under Union protection, it decided to set up what it called "contraband camps" to provide them with at least some meager support and shelter. Eventually it is estimated that some 100 camps were established in the South, in Union-occupied areas mainly on the Atlantic Coast, parts of the Mississippi valley, and southern Louisiana, with as many as perhaps 200,000 people in them by the end of the war, the only free black population except for those in the military. But conditions were desperately squalid. The soldiers assigned to tend to them generally resented such hated "babysitting:" "Many, very many of the soldiers and not a few of the officers," wrote a correspondent of the *New York Post*, "have habitually treated the negroes with the coarsest and most brutal insolence and humanity." Freedom was indeed bought at a severe price; a modern black historian has said that, "surrounded by squalor and harassed by Union soldiers, they were made to follow a code of conduct that hardly differed from the one that had characterized their bondage." So much for forty acres and a mule.

But at least those people had some modicum of emancipation. The bitter—and very seldom mentioned—truth is that the great majority of Southern blacks, nominally free, seem to have had lives that were in most ways much like they had had before the

Proclamation, though in many areas on plantations ravaged by the war. Taking the freed slaves who joined the Union forces and those who were contrabands — that would be around 300,000 people in all — it seems clear that most of the 3.5 million blacks in the South did not run to freedom, even if they did know of the Proclamation. How they led their lives is mostly a matter of speculation, since written accounts are few, but from several examples in scattered states it seems that most of them stayed on at the plantations where they had been enslaved, either growing food for themselves and their families or sometimes entering into contracts with whatever owners remained and hoping to be paid wages where the plantations could sell its commodities. Lincoln may have thought that he was granting freedom to the slaves, though he soon realized that he had done nothing really to ensure that. As late as August 1864, complaining that blacks "had not rallied" as he expected, he asked Frederick Douglass to somehow induce the freedmen to "come within Federal lines." No such way was found.

By November, eleven months after the proclamation, the Union had won several significant battles, including one on the fields of Pennsylvania near Gettysburg, where the Confederates had sought to engage Union forces to give the capital of Richmond some respite from Northern attacks but failed to penetrate the Union lines and had to retreat, suffering some 23,000 casualties (only a little more than the Union, it must be said). Four and a half months after the battle, Lincoln was asked to go to Gettysburg and dedicate a war memorial there. Now at his shrewdest, he took this opportunity to try to revise the whole purpose of the war and to provide the Northern soldiers and public — and history — with a cause that, instead of merely preserving the Union as had been generally understood until then, now took on the banners of equality and liberty that had been unfurled in the cause of black emancipation.

He began his distortion of history by declaring that "a new nation" had been created in 1776 (it was created in 1789, of course) so that he could make subtle reference to the Declaration of Independence and its assertion that all men are created equal, though his implication that it was part of the new nation—"a new nation, conceived in liberty, and dedicated to the proposition that all men are created equal"—was entirely false. In fact the Constitution that created that nation makes no mention of equality at all, and indeed it endorses the institution of slavery and provides for the return of fugitive slaves. As to liberty, that is mentioned in the preamble obliquely —"to secure the Blessings of Liberty"—but it comes seventh, after "more perfect Union," "Justice," "domestic Tranquility," "common Defense," and "general Welfare," suggesting that its role in the conception of the nation was minimal at best. And, unlike the others, it is not subsequently mentioned or provided for in the articles.

Lincoln goes on to call the ongoing conflict a "civil war," a convenient fiction which served to plant an idea of a threatened republic, but it was not a civil war—in true civil wars, as the English Civil Wars of the 17th century or the wars of the French Revolution (Vendee), one side seeks to remove the other from power and take over the state, which the Confederacy had no desire whatsoever to do. And he continues the heightened tone of the Southern threat by claiming that it is a war testing "the endurance" of the nation, which was true only in the sense that the South wanted to change the nature of it but not to threaten the existence of the Northern version of it.

Finally Lincoln gets around to "that cause" for which the soldiers honored at the memorial (only Union soldiers) had given their lives. It was, first, for "a new birth of freedom," presumably the freedom of the enslaved blacks and perhaps the freedom of the North to do whatever it wanted to do—neither of them ever understood by the general run of soldiers, certainly before the Proclamation, as being their purpose on the field. And second, to make sure a democratic government—of, by, and for "the people" —would not perish, as if that were the kind of government the Founding Fathers, whose fear of and aversion to democracy and the rule of mobs that it implies, had any intention of creating. That phrase, by the way, was taken by Lincoln from a sermon by a Boston abolitionist who had said that it defined democracy, so Lincoln well knew that he was using it in a context that the creators of the nation would have felt revulsion to.

That there was little or no applause at the end of the President's short speech was understandable given the quite unusual and unfamiliar cast he had given, unannounced and unexpected, to the Union cause which must have puzzled many and disturbed others. It was an instantly popular speech, however, and was reprinted often in the coming weeks, and it served, just as Lincoln hoped it would, to sanction the war in a new and high-moral way that the cause of preserving the Union had never done.

The terrible swift sword could now be unsheathed and held high and the righteous sentence proclaimed.

On April 24 of this year Lincoln issued an order drafted by Columbia University law professor Francis Lieber that codified the generally accepted universal standards of the common law of warfare, particularly as it related to the lives and property of civilians. Among its actions deemed to be criminal and prohibited were the "wanton devastation of a district," "infliction of suffering" on civilians, "murder of private citizens," "unnecessary or revengeful destruction of life," and "all wanton violence...all robbery, all pillage or sacking...all rape, wounding, maiming, or killing."

And yet it also provided, in its articles 14 and 15, a slippery provision called "military necessity," under which "destruction...of armed enemies" and of "other persons whose destruction is incidentally unavoidable" was completely permissible, and allowed "the appropriation of whatever an enemy's country affords" by the conquering army — provisions broad enough to cover a considerable amount of the very pillaging and sacking and maiming and killing it had earlier condemned. Broad enough, at any rate, for the Union generals now to enlarge the conflict in ways that General Hallek could say that spring changed "the character of the war" and allowed "no peace but that which is forced by the sword." General Ulysses Grant, now in charge of the Union's eastern army added that the goal was now "the complete subjugation of the South...destroying their means of subsistence...and in every other way possible."

The Union Army in the preceding years of the war had generally observed such principles as the Lieber Code set out, although there had been many instances of victorious troops that, as one general said of the Union troops in Baton Rouge, "regard pillaging not only right in itself but a soldierly accomplishment" and there were a few instances of renegade generals who led their troops into wholesale devastation of civilian targets. (Most famous perhaps was General J.H. Lane of Kansas whose men committed what is known as the Sacking of Osceola [Missouri] when in September 1861 the town of 3,000 was plundered and burnt to the ground, with nine civilians murdered.)

But when the new element to the war became the cause of eliminating of slavery, a certain moral fervor was cast upon the troops, or a good many of them at least, that eventually added a kind of John-Brown-like zealotry to the Union cause. It was not that there was any particular passion to see black people freed but rather to abolish slavery itself, an easily condemnable institution that was the economic and political pillar of the hated Southerners. That is why, within just a few months of the Proclamation, a number of commanders in the field, despite the recently released Lieber code, felt sanctioned to unleash the equivalent of what in the 20th century came to be called "total war" — a war upon civilians and their property in the South, with attendant looting, murder, arson, and rape. Neither women, children, the old and infirm, or oftentimes even blacks, were spared. As General-in-Chief Hallek noted in a letter to Ulysses Grant on March 31, 1863:

The character of the war has very much changed. There is now no possible hope of reconciliation with the rebels...There can be no peace but that which is forced by the sword. We must conquer the rebels.

A few days later Grant concurred:

Rebellion has assumed that shape now that it can only terminate by the complete subjugation of the South...It is our duty to weaken the enemy, by destroying their means of subsistence, withdrawing their means of cultivating their fields, and in every other way possible.

Thus it was that in his campaign in the West against Vicksburg, Mississippi, in the Spring and Summer of 1863, Grant had no compunction in attacking civilians and destroying feed mills: "Civilians were suffering from unceasing bombardment and the shortage of food," both violations of the Lieber Code. In the aftermath, Grant ordered General William Sherman east to Jackson, the capital of Mississippi, which he conquered on July 17 after five days of incessant bombardment without Confederate resistance and proceeded to unleash the troops on a three-day rampage that, according to a Northern reporter, "left the entire business section in ruins, burned most of the better residences...and looted homes, churches, and the state library," leading a fellow journalist to say that "such complete ruin and devastation never followed the footsteps of any army before." Sherman boasted to Grant, "The land is devastated for 30 miles around."

Sherman's next target was Meridian, an important rail center with a Confederate arsenal and military hospital, which he entered in February 1864, and although again without resistance, again unleashed his troops against civilian targets. "I...began systematic and thorough destruction," he reported to Grant. "For five days 10,000 men worked hard and with a will in that work of destruction, with axes, crowbars, sledges, clawbars, and with fire, and I have no hesitation in pronouncing the work as well done. Meridian, with its depts., store-houses, arsenal, hospitals, offices, hotels, and cantonments no longer exists." The railway was destroyed, 115 miles of tracks laid waste and 66 bridges left in ruins.

Planning a sweep into Georgia, Sherman dispatched troops under General Kenner Garrard into Roswell, a mill town about twenty miles north of Atlanta. The soldiers burned the mills, then received orders from Sherman to arrest the owners and the women employees of the mills "and send them, under guard, charged with treason, to Marietta...whence I will send them by cars to the North." Such kidnapping went well beyond the Lieber code, of course, but some 500 women and children, after being kept out in the open square for a week, were eventually shipped North, and it is thought that in the end some 2,000 destitute and innocent civilians in the next few months were shipped by Sherman north of the Ohio to fend for themselves, most taking on menial jobs where they could.

In September Sherman began his famed "march to the sea" — the first out-and-out demonstration of scorched-earth war — with the conquest of Atlanta, which the smaller Confederate forces vainly tried to defend. Sherman set out the strategy in a letter to Hallek that September: "Until we can repopulate Georgia, it is useless to occupy it, but the utter destruction of its roads, houses, and people will cripple their military resources. I can...make Georgia howl." And a few months later: "We are not only fighting hostile armies, but a hostile people, and must make old and young, rich and poor, feel the hard hand of war, as well as their organized armies." So he ordered the evacuation of the city and the burning of the greater part of it — only 400 of some 4,000 private homes were left standing — while his soldiers looted and pillaged all that they could, including churches and graveyards.

Then in November began the march of plunder and pillage south and east to Savannah, 60,000 men on a rampage for two months, taking or destroying foodstores, looting anything of value before usually burning plantations, warehouses, private homes, and roadside shacks, raping women both white and black, then setting fire in a swath up to 60 miles wide. A young woman, Eliza Andrews, described the scenes she came on just after Sherman's army had passed through:

> We struck the "Burnt Country," as it is well-named by the natives, and then I could better understand the wrath and desperation of these poor people...There was hardly a fence left standing all the way from Sparta to Gordon [35 miles]. The fields were trampled down and the road was lined with the carcasses of horses, hogs, and cattle that the invaders...had wantonly shot down to starve out the people and prevent them from making their crops. The stench in some places was unbearable...The dwellings that were standing all showed signs of pillage, and on every plantation we saw the charred remains of the [cotton] gin house and packing screw, where here and there the lone chimney stacks, "Sherman's Sentinels," told of homes laid in ashes.

Sherman himself estimated that his army did $100 million of damage to the countryside—something over $.4 billion today—and destroyed 300 miles of railway, capturing 5,000 horses and 13,000 head of cattle and leaving the population destitute.

In the course of his rampage, Sherman acquired, little liking it, about 25,000 free blacks—the "contrabands"—who fled to the Northern army in hopes of being fed and sheltered. In fact, Sherman tried to discourage these hangers-on, for they placed a serious burden on the troops' supplies, all of which had to be scavenged from the countryside, and only a few of the men were useful as labor since their skills were limited. In the end fewer than 7,000 blacks made it all the way to the coast, though there Sherman issued a field order that land within 30 miles of the coast could be turned over to them in

40-acre plots so that they wouldn't continue to depend upon the Union supplies.

The siege of Savannah itself just before Christmas was short, the mayor suing for peace after a few days of shelling, with the Confederate troops, outnumbered and outgunned, leaving the city and heading north. Sherman spared the city the kind of destruction meted out elsewhere while he resupplied his men from the Union ships that had blockaded the Savannah harbor and from plantation fields in the area. They stayed about a month, preparing for another swath of scorched earth northward in South Carolina. As Sherman wrote to Hallek once he settled in Savannah, "The truth is the whole army is burning with an insatiable desire to wreck vengeance upon South Carolina. I almost tremble at her fate, but feel that she deserves all that seems in store for her."

That campaign was, unbelievably, even fiercer than the Georgia one, for after all South Carolina had been the first to secede and first to fire a shot (though in answer to a Union invasion of Charleston Harbor); a reporter for a Northern newspaper wrote: "As for wholesale burning, pillage, devastation, committed in South Carolina, magnify all I have said of Georgia fifty-fold, and then throw in an occasional murder."

The army, still 60,000 strong, marched north through the state in two swaths, one going up the coast toward Charleston and the larger unit going northwest to Columbia, the capital, where the vengeance it planned was indeed insatiable, and on into North Carolina. Resistance was meager, there being not more than a few thousand able-bodied soldiers left in the whole state. Destruction of property, military and civilian, through the countryside was nonetheless total: a Union captain wrote that "the destruction of houses, barns, mills, etc. was almost universal," and a Sherman aide testified that "a majority of the Cities, towns, villages and country houses have been burnt to the ground," many of which were never rebuilt even after the war. A Union major, George Nichols, wrote this condemnation: "Aside from the destruction of military things, there were destructions overwhelming, overleaping the present generation...agriculture, commerce, cannot be revived in our day. Day by day our legions of armed men surged over the land, over a region forty miles wide, burning everything we could not take away." At least 35 towns and cities in South Carolina, and an unknown number of plantations, were torched and destroyed.

A Captain George Pepper classified the devastations:

> First, "deliberate and systematic robbery for the sake of gain." Thousands of soldiers have gathered by violence hundreds of dollars each, some of them thousands, by sheer robbery.... This robbery extends to other valuables in addition to money. Plate and silver spoons, silk dresses, elegant articles of the toilet, pistols, indeed whatever the soldier can take away and hopes to sell...

> A second form of devastation...consisted in the "wanton destruction of property which they could not use or carry away."...This robbery and wanton waste were specially trying to the people, not only because contrary to right and the laws of war, but because it completed their utter and almost hopeless impoverishment. The depth of their losses and present want can hardly be overstated.

The devastation of Barnwell, 80 miles northwest of Savannah, seems to have been typical. South Carolina literary light William Gilmore Simms would write:

> On what plea was the picturesque village of Barnwell destroyed? We had no army there for its defense: no issue of strength in its neighborhood had excited the passions of its combatants. Yet it was plundered — and nearly all burned to the ground; and this, too, where

the town was occupied by women and children only. So, too, the fate of Blackville, Graham, Bamberg, Buford's Bridge, Lexington, etc., all hamlets of most modest character, where no resistance was offered — where no fighting took place — where there was no provocation of liquor even, and where the only exercise of heroism was at the expense of women, infancy, and feebleness.

A Mrs. Aldrich remembered the sight of Barnwell after the Union army left:

> All the public buildings were destroyed. The fine brick Courthouse, with most of the stores, laid level with the ground, and many private residences with only the chimneys standing like grim sentinels; the Masonic Hall in ashes. I had always believed that the archives, jewels and sacred emblems of the Order were so reverenced by Masons everywhere... that those wearing the "Blue" would guard the temple of their brothers in "Gray." Not so, however: Nothing in South Carolina was held sacred.

All this was exceeded by Sherman's obliteration of Columbia, which his army reached in mid-February 1865, and though the city surrendered without resistance Sherman set his troops loose to pillage and burn the hated center of secession, the soldiers "infuriated, cursing, screaming, exulting in their work," according to one account. It goes on: "The drunken devils roamed about, setting fire to every house the flames seemed likely to spare...They would enter houses and in the presence of helpless women and children, pour turpentine on the beds and set them on fire." By midnight "the whole town was wrapped in one huge blaze."

Simms draws these pictures:

Hardly had the troops reached the head of Main street, when the first work of pillage began. Stores were broken open within the first hour after their arrival, and gold, silver, jewels and liquors eagerly sought... Among the first fires at evening was one about dark, which broke out in a filthy purlieu of low houses of wood on Gervais street, occupied mostly as brothels... Almost at the same time a body of the soldiers scattered over the eastern outskirts of the city fired severally the dwellings... There were then some twenty fires in full blast, in as many different quarters...thus enveloping in flames almost every section of the devoted city... By midnight, Main street, from its northern to its southern extremity, was a solid wall of fire... And while these scenes were at their worst—while the flames were at their highest and most extensively ranging—groups might be seen at the several corners of the streets, drinking, roaring, reveling—while the fiddle and accordion were playing their popular airs among them.

And this was not the happenstantial work of a few renegade soldiers. This was what Sherman intended giving loose to his army's "insatiable desire." In his memoirs he bluntly bragged that he had "utterly ruined Columbia."

On March 3, Sherman's troops had captured the little city of Florence, in northern South Carolina, on their way to North Carolina. A Union officer, noting the army's path, wrote: "The sufferings which the people will have to undergo will be most intense. We have left on the wide strip of country we have passed over no provisions which will go any distance in supporting the people." On that same day, 350 miles north, Abraham Lincoln addressed a crowd from the steps of the capitol after his second inauguration. He promised to continue the war being fought "with malice toward none; with charity for all." With malice toward none.

The next month, in Virginia, at General Grant's headquarters,

Sherman regaled Lincoln with reports on his successful marches through the South. He recalled in his memoirs that the President was particularly keen on his stories of the foragers in uniform and their pillaging and burning as they wreaked their vengeance on the enemy, or at least the enemy's countryside and civilian population.

Sherman's campaign, along with those of General Philip Sheridan in the Shenandoah Valley (where he followed out Grant's instructions to leave it "a barren waste") and Grant's in Virginia against Lee's declining forces, had their desired effect. The Confederacy's back was effectively broken, and with burnt-out fields, decimated livestock, devastated populations, and no slave labor under control it was left without means to recover and regroup. On April 9 Lee surrendered to Grant at Appomattox and within a month or so other Confederate commands followed suit.

As was said in another context, they made a desert and called it peace.

In the end, after four years of brutal war, the bloodiest in American history, the first to be fought on civilian soil, the South had lost at least 50,000 civilians, by the commonly reckoned account, mostly to disease and starvation but not a few to weaponry. Another 426,000 soldiers died, at a bare minimum, maybe 30 per cent of white males of military age in the South, and some 320,000 were wounded; suicide and mental illness amounted to what SUNY Binghamton scholar Diane Miller Sommerville has called "a virtual epidemic of emotional and psychiatric trauma among Confederate soldiers and veterans." The South suffered an estimated $3.3 billion in property damage, including railroads, bridges (one third said to be destroyed), banks, factories, warehouses, and homes. And some 3.5 million slaves, reckoned in 1860 to be worth $3.5 billion in 1860 (in 1860 dollars, $10 trillion today), were taken from their owners, what historian R. R. Palmer has called "an annihilation of individual property rights without parallel...in the history of the modern world," no people anywhere having "to face such a total and overwhelming loss of property values as the slave-owners of the American South."

If the estimate of the total cost of the war is accurate — put at $6.6 billion by the *Encyclopedia of the Confederacy*, $22.6 trillion today — then the South would have paid the much greater part of that, and yet with an infrastructure demolished in most places it had no real means of recovery. All of its prewar railroads were destroyed (except for the Louisville & Nashville, which the Union Army used), and even as late as 1880 the South had only a third of its prewar mileage. Its entire economy, almost entirely based on plantation agriculture, was destroyed, and even where farming was taken up again it was mostly done by sharecroppers now. The North, which expanded its manufacturing and railroad sectors threefold during the war years, hardly suffered at all and was able in the war's aftermath to build a prosperous infrastructure for the future.

But the toll on the South was far greater even than the huge number of people lost and the devastated landscape. For the South was a conquered country, whipped, disheartened, demoralized, beaten in soul and spirit, its social fabric in tatters, its customs and traditions trampled on, its institutions gutted, and its very civilization shaken to its roots. The *Nation* magazine, a pro-Union publication that started this year, wrote in September: "There has probably never been a people, since the Gauls, so thoroughly beaten in war as the Southerners have been... This generation is certainly as the mercy of its conqueror, and incapable of offering the least opposition to its mandates."

In December 1865, three Unionist-run governments in Alabama, North Carolina, and Georgia became the final three states to approve the Thirteenth Amendment, outlawing slavery, and so assuring that it became law. It did nothing, of course, to provide another social and economic role for the formerly enslaved, or to have any regard for the deprivation of the former slave owners, but its purpose was in fact more punitive than practical, and it enshrined the principles of the Emancipation Proclamation, limited as they were, in the Constitution.

Lincoln was not alive at the time, having been assassinated eight months before, but he had supported the amendment vigorously, logrolling the House shamelessly to get its vote in favor, knowing that the terms of the Proclamation, as a specifically war measure, would not survive legal challenges after the war. However inadequate in fact, this would serve as his grandest memorial.

One irony in the amendment: though its language reads that slavery shall not exist "within the United States, or any place subject to *their* jurisdiction," that plural reading of the components of the Union had effectively been demolished, never to have meaning again, by a war that established a unitary polity governed from Washington that put an end, in all practical senses, to the idea of independent, sovereign states and individual states' rights. There was to be one country, indivisible, and hereafter the language it uses is, fittingly, "the United States *is*."

III. Reconstruction and Destruction, 1866-1877

I T IS IMPOSSIBLE TO SAY what would have happened in the process of restoring the Southern states to the Union if Lincoln had lived, but it is fair to assume that it would have been far smoother, and fairer, than it came to be after Vice President Andrew Johnson acceded to the Presidency in April 1865. For one thing Lincoln had a fairly efficient working relationship with Congress, able to keep the Radical Republicans more or less under control, and though he never adequately spelled it out, he had several ideas about the restoration of the union and the future of the black freed population that might have won the day. At the core of his proposed reconstruction was the idea of conciliation toward the South, easy paths to re-entry, a limited black franchise, and possible colonization of freedmen – all of which were espoused by Johnson once in office, but futilely, for he had no influence in Congress and no real personal following (except in his home state of Tennessee) to provide him with political clout.

Hence not one of these was ever considered for a moment by the triumphant Radical Republicans once Lincoln was gone, nor was there much support for them among the Republican press or Republican circles in the states. As a result, the period known as "Reconstruction," from 1865 to 1877, turned instead into a period of vast and calamitous *de*construction throughout the South, a dozen years that served to sour race relations and condemn the South to backwardness for the next hundred years.

In September of 1865, six months after Congress created a Freedmen's Bureau as an arm of (oddly) the War Department to be the overseer of the 3 million free blacks in the South, providing jobs, schooling, medical care, and perhaps land, a distinguished Virginia clergyman and academic named Robert L. Dabney wrote a long letter (published the next month in the *New York Weekly News*) to Major General Oliver O. Howard, chief of the Bureau in Washington, concerning its "dealing with the African race in these United States."

After spelling out the immense new powers the Bureau was given—its agents could arrest any freed slave and transport him to industries anywhere else for compulsory labor, it had military-style courts of its own for freedmen superseding civil courts in every city and county in eleven Southern states—Dabney pointed out its obligation with such great powers "to do good to your charge upon a great scale" and with as much zeal as it had showed waging "a gigantic war" for four years. And "if a change procured for the Africans at such a cost brings them no actual benefits," then the war "was a blunder and a crime."

As to the kind of benefits, Dabney argued that "the very best you can do for them must be more than the South has accomplished," and he proceeded to list what that has been: first, assuring "the physical welfare of the negro," evidenced by increasing population and longevity rates and a declining rate of illness, without poverty or destitution anywhere and with provisions for illness and old age everywhere; second, seeing that all blacks learned English and "tens of thousands" were taught to read, plus many men learned mechanical arts and most women learned "domestic arts"; third, providing a rich spiritual life through Christianity, with religious instruction standard and blacks invited to white churches where they were not provided churches of their own. "My argument," he concluded, "is that you must do more for the negro than we sinners of the South have done… If the South, with all its disadvantages, has done this modicum of good to this poor people, the North, their present guardians, with their vast advantages, must do far more."

And it must be the North that does this, for "the South cannot." It is now "utterly impoverished," and besides, since the North has taught the blacks and convinced them that "the white people of the South were their oppressors and enemies," now they "will no longer listen to the Southern people" and the North can no longer count on the eight million white people, "among whom alone are to be found persons familiar with the African character," to guide or counsel or instruct them.

Then, professing not to believe any such thing himself, Dabney notes that the critics of the North are saying that in fact it wants "the ruin of the African" and to see him "perish like the red man," so that Northern interests can "take the land he occupied." And he warns, "You must refute this monstrous indictment" by assuring greater prosperity for the blacks than the South has provided, or else the world will see that it is really true and amounts to "the blackest public crime of the nineteenth century," one that will condemn blacks to "destitution, degradation, immorality" for generations to come. It will not be easy, it may take "a million people and three-thousand million dollars," it will have to overcome the hostility to whites that the North has generated, and it will not have the aid of 280,000 slave owners who are on the spot, but it is "a sacred obligation" that if the North fails to meet "it confesses itself an enormous criminal."

Finally, Dabney darkly warns that this obligation in fact is unprecedented: the North has "to do what no other mortal has done successfully, to transmute four millions of slaves, of an alien race and lower culture, all at once into citizens, without allowing them to suffer or deteriorate on your hands...a social revolution new in the history of man."

It is not recorded that Dabney ever received a reply to this letter, and that is hardly to be wondered at. For General Howard, and assuredly those around him in the Bureau, knew perfectly well that the task of merely feeding and clothing the freedmen in need was proving daunting enough, much less finding them jobs and schools, and as things were going in a still-chaotic South there would seem to be no way that the North could live up to Dabney's charge.

"Reconstruction" was a process largely directed by a Congress that, after the election of 1866, was entirely in the hands of the Radical Republicans led by Pennsylvania Representative Thaddeus Stevens and Massachusetts Senator Charles Sumner. Johnson, who opposed them and often vetoed their measures, was repeatedly overridden in both houses and in February of 1868 was even impeached by them, a move that lost by only one vote in the Senate.

The Radical Republican's triumphant strategy was simple, and for most of a dozen years it operated as the law of the land: Revenge, Republicans, and Reconstruction.

As for the first, it was well expressed by Stevens: "We must revolutionize Southern institutions, habits, and manners... The foundation of their institutions...must be broken up and relaid, or all our blood and treasure have been spent in vain." The South was in ruins from the war and should remain that way, leaving the way clear for Northern entrepreneurs and land speculators as well as enough blacks to see to it that Republicans got elected to office. Southern whites were to remain powerless as far as possible—the Military Reconstruction Acts of 1867 and 1868 even denied suffrage to white men unless they took an oath of allegiance to the Union, and the

Fourteenth Amendment in 1868 denied public office to anyone who had "engaged in insurrection" — and military administrations, run by Union soldiers with black militias, were to operate Southern state governments and create new states that would seek readmission to the Union. Stevens acknowledged that all this was Congress operating "outside" the Constitution and at one point admitted that it did look as if "our whole work of reconstruction were usurpation."

The military governments' first task was to oversee elections, everywhere designed of course to put Republicans in office, thus assuring Republican domination in Congress for years to come and a carrying-through of the party's national agenda of public financing of railroads, a pro-business banking system, and high protective tariffs for industry. In statewide elections they could count on the support of the freed blacks, whom the Radicals had given universal male suffrage without conditions, over the objections of a great many, including a great many in the North and Border who mightily resisted any such suffrage there (Ohio, Kansas, and Missouri defeated black suffrage referendums in the 1867 elections). Especially including Johnson, who was deeply worried that it would trigger racial enmity for generations; as he told Frederick Douglass after a black delegation urged unconditional suffrage in a meeting at the White House in January 1886: "The query comes up whether these two races...without preparation, without time for passion and excitement to be appeased, and without time for the slightest improvement, whether the one should be turned loose upon the other at the ballot box with this enmity and hate existing between them...whether we do not commence a war of races."

The Radicals, all of them Northerners with scant personal knowledge of the South, considered such fears exaggerated, overrode Johnson's veto, and went ahead with universal suffrage in the South (blacks in most Northern states had no vote) without much regard for the consequences as long as they could count on freed slaves voting for Lincoln's party. And to assure that blacks would indeed vote the proper way, the Union Leagues of New York and Philadelphia, working as an arm of the Republican Party, sent organizers in black neighborhoods throughout the South as early as the spring of 1865 and formed secret black societies and even armed black militias that at one point numbered at least 200,000 men. Hence in every Southern state but Tennessee (which had already had a Union-army government and returned to the Union) constitutional conventions were held in 1866 and 1867, dominated by Republicans white and black, to create new states outlawing slavery, with Republican governors and legislatures that would ask re-admittance to the Union and send representatives to Congress.

As to Reconstruction—the recreation of sovereign, stable states that could return to the Union on equal footing with the rest of the nation—that was not ever a primary task of government, as the Radicals saw it. In their eyes revenge and Republicanism were primary, and the return of states to the Union could be adequately done by the coalition of freed black males and the horde of Northern whites—carpetbaggers, they were generally called—who descended on the South after the war to advance their individual fortunes in societies so shattered that a later historian called it a land of "destitution, desolation, utter hopelessness." So the Republican governments that were established, under the guide of the Union army, consisted mostly of shrewd Northern opportunists (and a few Southern opportunists, called scalawags in some quarters) and a few revenge-minded blacks that proceeded to dominate the white populations, increasing taxes, creating black schools (at an ultimate cost of almost $2 million), integrating such services as streetcars and theaters, selling land to railroad speculators, and siphoning off state treasuries for gubernatorial and legislative salaries and perks. This, on top of the judicial system and land allotment being in the hands of Freedmen's Bureau agents (who eventually took over 2 million farms, mostly for Northern speculators), the Treasury Department using agents to confiscate plantation lands they deemed to be derelict, and a Union occupation army free to take over the best houses and buildings, left whites, already in sorry economic straits, generally poor and powerless throughout the South. "Utter ruin and abject degradation are our portion," as one Southerner put it in 1866. The London *Telegraph* observed, "Eight million of the people are subjects, not citizens."

Perhaps it is not surprising, given the chaos out of which these new state governments were created and the largely unsupervised ways in which they operated, that every single one was, to one degree or another, mired in theft, bribery, fraud, dishonesty, and corruption. (It didn't help that for most of this period the Federal government was, too, and many cities in the North, but that's another story.)

Reconstruction began with the elections for delegates to state constitutional conventions in 1867-69, in which blacks played a significant part everywhere, even a majority in North and South Carolina and Virginia, along with heavy participation of carpetbaggers and a few Southern whites. In every place, since the state was paying for the conventions, delegates awarded themselves hefty expenses and bonuses, and in several places they established free bars in the capitols. In Florida, the convention issued $50,000 in script, $15,000 distributed to the delegates immediately, with $10,000 for the president; the North Carolina convention cost $100,000, Mississippi's $250,000. All but Georgia's wrote constitutions that limited the white vote, enfranchised blacks, provided for some integration of public services, and created state school systems, which generally meant all-black schools and colleges. A sense of how Southern whites generally reacted to all this comes from a South Carolinian who said he would not obey the new laws because they came from "a negro constitution, of a negro government, establishing negro equality" and did not apply to him—and where such feelings of disaffection and illegitimacy prevailed among great portions of the population it was inevitable that there would be no effective governance and for the most part no peace for the next decade.

The governments thus created all held elections for their legislatures and in most cases for governors and Congressmen. Whites in general (except for Republicans, usually carpetbaggers) boycotted these elections and the Union League worked diligently to get out the black vote, so the resulting governments were again made up of blacks, carpetbaggers, and scalawags in various proportions, overwhelmingly Republican for the most part. The fact that the governments were representative of only half or less of the population, were installed without any mandate, and had no constituencies to answer to (since they answered to the Union army) meant that there were no barriers to open graft and corruption, which were practiced by both races with ingenuity and enthusiasm throughout their reign.

Let's look at some of them.

South Carolina was not exactly a typical Southern state, since blacks were a slight majority of the population and blacks were effectively in charge of the government from 1868 to 1875, though there was a white governor throughout. And corruption may have been worse there than anywhere else in the South: by 1870 the *Nation* magazine could say that the state was "almost completely at the mercy of black and white corruptionists." But its style of chicanery was very much like that of other states.

For example, the legislature created a ring of Republican newspapers and guided state treasure to them, effectively establishing a party network with a reach easily outperforming the white press: the state's printing bill increased from $21,000 in 1868 to $450,000 in 1873. In Columbia, the *Daily Record* billed the government $17,174 for printing services and received nearly $60,000 and the *Charleston Republican* billed $24,538 and got $60,982, the money normally being split with the legislators from those districts. Additional sums were acquired by arranging for the 35 legislative staffers to get pay vouchers, then actually issuing vouchers for 350, thus helping to pay for local Republican officials back home. The legislature allotted more than $200,000 for refurnishing the State House in Columbia (including 200 cuspidors for the 124 members), but in the end only $18,000 worth of furnishings was actually installed, the rest presumably going to the members' local houses and their favorite haunts. And in 1869, the legislature voted to pay $75,000 to have a state census taken, even though the Federals were slated to take one the following year — and that one was done for just $43,000.

The corruption was so notorious that it eventually even attracted the attention of the Northern press: the *New York Times* in 1874 dismissed the state government as "a gang of thieves."

Alabama was no less corrupt, again largely in the control of blacks in the state legislature, helped by a series of carpet-bagging white governors. A Republican leader in 1870 was notorious for having gotten $35,000 for seeing through a railroad bond, but in fact every state in the South at this time was being corrupted by (mostly Northern) railroad interests, ultimately creating state debts from 1866 to 1872 of $132 million in railroad stocks and bonds. A Democratic politician, General James Clanton, complained that "in the statehouse and out of it, bribes were offered and accepted at noonday, and without hesitation or shame." Additional money came to the state through a flagrant scheme of increasing taxes on white-owned property, backed by Treasury agents and the occupying Union army, eventually assessing four times as much in 1872 as it did in 1865 and forcing a number of families into bankruptcy.

One typical scheme unfolded one spring when the U.S. Congress allocated $80,000 for flood relief after a brutal storm left many, black and white, homeless and hungry. The Alabama Republican party, which controlled the funds, used them to hold a series of church dinners, in black areas only, mostly nowhere near the flood-ravaged villages, and only where it was promised that the congregations would vote Republican.

Finally, a look at *Georgia,* and here we have the words of a contemporary, Democratic Representative Dan Vorhees of Indiana, who in a speech to the House in 1872 lambasted the Radical Republicans for their treatment of the South, particularly Georgia:

> Let the great state of Georgia speak first... You clung to her throat; you battered her features out of shape and recognition, determined that your party should have undisputed possession and enjoyment of her offices, her honors, and her substance. Then bound hand and foot you handed her over to the rapacity of robbers...

> In 1861 Georgia was free from debt. Taxes were light as air... Her credit stood high, and when the war closed she was still free from indebtedness. After six years of Republican rule you present her, to the horror of the world, loaded with a debt of $50 million, and the crime against Georgia is the crime this same party has committed against the other Southern States... Rufus B. Bullock [from New York], Governor of Georgia [1868-71]...served three years and then absconded with all of the gains. The Legislature of two years spent $100,000 more than had been spent during any eight previous years. They even put the children's money, laid aside for education of white and black, into their own pockets."

In one sense, it is not really surprising that the governments of the Southern states should engage in what was little more than looting for as long as they could. In addition to there being no institutions or constituencies that could exercise oversight or control, the blacks in power inevitably felt some sense of retribution and compensation due them for past injustice, and the whites, both the Northerners who had no loyalty to Southern turf and the Southerners who joined the enemy, were there precisely for personal gain. It took some time for the majority of white Southerners, beaten down in so many ways by the war defeat, to figure out means to react and eventually recreate the Democratic Party, organize, and return to power.

The initial response of white Southerners to the Union army occupation and its use of armed black troops to establish order across the South was to express outrage and to appeal to the military commanders to exert more control over the often wayward platoons, which operated without much discipline; South Carolina's Wade Hampton, who had been a lieutenant general in the Confederate army, complained to Jackson as early as the fall of 1865 about "your brutal negro troops under their no less brutal and more degraded Yankee officers [by whom] the grossest outrages were committed...with impunity." Yet most commanders were indifferent to the troops' behavior, as long as they served to keep whites in line and were useful in getting black freedmen to the polls. In the 1870 elections, black militiamen were used freely to intimidate populations where the Democrats were strongest—some 7,000 were set loose in South Carolina alone—and to see to it that blacks participated fully in the campaigns and the balloting.

The other means to these ends was the concerted effort by the Union Leagues, backed by considerable Northern money, to create black societies, frequently armed, in every Southern state, both to protect blacks' newly won rights (particularly after the enactment of the Civil Rights Bill and the 14th amendment in 1866) and to prevent plantation owners from imposing slavery on the workers, a great many of whom had no land of their own—all the promises of 40 acres and a mule proving empty—and continued to work for their former masters for wages, though usually living off the plantation and not in the former slave quarters. The Union League of New York boasted of creating as many as 120 black societies in Louisiana alone; North Carolina was said to have enrolled 80,000 freedmen.

Exactly what these black societies did is a matter of some dispute—some argue they acted only when threatened by

43

unresponsive whites, others (such as an English visitor, Robert Summers) that they caused "a real reign of terror among the whites" — the response of whites in many places in the South was to create white secret societies of their own, the most important of which was the Ku Klux Klan, started in Tennessee in December 1865. In the following year it spread to all the Southern states, though initially it was designed more for defense against Federal troops and black societies than as an offensive weapon. It attracted at the beginning a great number of respectable men of position and was led by generals from the Confederacy (e.g., James Clanton in Alabama, James George in Mississippi, John Gordon in Georgia), who sought to create an intimidating military force that, using secrecy and disguise, would deter any black interference; General Nathan Bedford Forrest, a war hero, was made its leader in 1867 and pledged that it would act as a "protective organization." That it surely was in many places, but in many places too it was inevitable to attract white followers of lesser stature and they often had little allegiance to the formal Klan organization. So many unauthorized Klan groups sprang up, committing raids and assaults in black populations, including beatings and in some few places killings, that Forrest in the fall of 1869 issued a denunciation of these groups and ordered that the organization would cease using its white hoods so that the bogus Klansmen could be recognized and deterred. That had little effect anywhere, and the lawlessness continued off and on in many places, provoking many states (Tennessee, South Carolina, North Carolina, and Georgia among them) to form state militias (normally poor whites with a smattering of blacks) to combat and suppress them, which they did with their own predictable violence and thuggery.

It was in this atmosphere that black-white clashes took place in many parts of the South, sometimes with beatings and killings of both whites and (mostly) blacks, leading the U.S. Congress to intervene in 1870 and create a committee to investigate the KKK, and create legislation to control it. The committee's hearings brought in hundreds of witnesses whose testimony eventually filled thirteen volumes, and the Republican majority afterward crafted legislation that would greatly expand Federal power by letting state crimes like robbery and assault be tried in Federal courts and authorizing the President to declare martial law and suspend habeas corpus wherever he wished to install military rule over areas of Klan activity. That was to be expected, but what is especially interesting is the report of the minority on the committee, which sought to put the rise of the Klan in some perspective:

> Had there been no tyrannical, corrupt, carpetbagger or Scalawag rule, there would have been no secret organizations. From the oppression and corruption of the one sprang the vice and outrage of the other... When, in secret sworn [black] organizations, hatred of the white race was instilled into the minds of these ignorant people [by the Union Leagues]...when the blacks were formed into military organizations and the white people of these states were denied the use of arms...in short, when the [white] people saw that they had no rights which were respected, no protection from insults, no security even for their wives and little children, and that what little they had saved from the ravages of war was being confiscated by taxation...many of them took the law into their own hands and did deeds of violence which we neither justify nor excuse. But all history shows that bad government will make bad citizens and when the corruption and villainy of the governments which Congress has set up and maintained over the Southern states are thoroughly understood...the world will be amazed at the long suffering and endurance of that people.

And these were all Northerners, mind; there were no Southern Democrats in Congress.

After the anti-Klan Act passed in April 1871, there was in fact a decline in Klan activity in most of the South, gradually replaced by a feeling that only a strengthening of the Democratic Party and an electoral strategy tied to white participation and power would provide long-term resistance to the overweening Republican rule. This was first manifest in the 1872 elections, in which the Democratic ticket for President won in Georgia, Tennessee, and Texas (and Kentucky) — its only wins in the country — and Democrats won state offices in those states and a few others. Efforts were stepped up for 1874 and Democrats fared even better in that fall's elections, in part because the Republicans were blamed for the crash of 1873 and the following depression that turned the sluggish economy of the South even more lethargic and because by now the multiple scandals in Washington had badly tarnished the reputation of President Grant and his colleagues. In the South Democrats in most states worked hard at organizing and mobilizing the white vote — in Mississippi, according to a Republican official there, "The Democrats were bold, outspoken, defiant, and determined" — and just as hard at intimidating black and Republican voters, often showing up at Republican campaign rallies with armed white gangs (usually ad hoc rather than Klan-inspired) and later trying to keep many of them from the polls. And so the Democrats nationally won control of the House, with strong Democratic victories in Texas, Arkansas, Tennessee, Virginia, and Georgia, and several seats in Louisiana, Mississippi, and Alabama. Thus the white Southern strategy to revivify the Democratic Party, helped along by armed white bands, began to bear fruit.

That strategy, if so it may be called, was continued over the next two years, one way or the other in all the Southern states, most dramatically in Virginia, Georgia, Tennessee, Texas, Arkansas, South Carolina, Alabama, and Louisiana.

In 1875 in South Carolina, for example, the Democrats organized from a statewide executive committee down to the precincts and chose General Wade Hampton, a military hero popular with the white population, for governor. Hampton made overtures to the blacks, without success, and tried to play down violence with a policy of "force without violence," trying to get the white bands to march but not attack the Republicans, also without much success. That summer black armed "Loyal Leagues" were formed across the state and there were armed conflicts in Aiken County (one white and seven blacks killed) and Charleston County (one white killed and at least 30 blacks captured and executed), showing that neither the state militia or armed blacks were capable of defending Republicans, and Hampton gave up his idea of a peaceful campaign; that fall, in fact, he was accompanied on his campaign tours through the state by armed mounted men dressed in red shirts who disrupted Republican meetings and tried to intimidate black voters.

With both sides armed and a crucial election at stake it was inevitable that there would be violence throughout the campaign. In Aiken County in September two black men robbed a white farm house, one was captured but the other fled to a black area where he was protected by Loyal Leaguers and when whites tried to deliver an arrest warrant shots were exchanged and what onlookers called a race war raged for three days before Federal troops arrived and dispersed both sides, but not before one white man was killed and thirty-nine black. It wasn't more than a month later in the town of Cainhoy that a meeting of white Democrats was set upon by armed blacks who killed six and suffered only one death when whites retaliated. A further confrontation was averted only when Federal troops arrived.

Federal soldiers were stationed throughout the state and Election Day went off that fall with little violence, and the Democrats eked out a victory — which the Republicans refused to accept. Thus both parties went to Columbia in November, both set up gubernatorial offices and legislatures, but while the Republicans had troop support the Democrats had all the authority and most of the money, because whites refused to pay regular taxes that would go to

Republican coffers and donated instead to the Hamptonites; as historian Walter Edgar put it, "The Reconstruction regime in South Carolina had lost what little authority and legitimacy it had" and "no one paid [it] any taxes or any mind."

A similar pattern played out in Mississippi, where blacks controlled the legislature, raising taxes every year on the white landowners until they were fourteen times as high in 1874 as they had been in 1869, and the carpetbagger governor was installed in office in 1874 only because General Sherman, in charge of the Fifth Military District, sent in troops to support him and deny Democrats office.

As elsewhere, this prompted whites to organize semi-military Democratic clubs (Red Shirts) to oppose the governor's armed black bands and launch a full-scale campaign in 1874-75 called the Mississippi Plan, with a three-pronged strategy: first to persuade or intimidate white voters (and blacks where possible) to switch from the Republican to the Democratic side, then to intimidate blacks so they would not campaign, register, or vote, and finally to use force to break up Republican meetings through the campaign. As a later Congressional committee would put it, "force, fraud, and intimidation were used generally and successfully," and in January 1875 there was a Democratic landslide. The Republican governor, threatened with impeachment, resigned, and the eight-year reign of the carpetbaggers was over.

There was nothing pleasant in the restoration of the Democratic regimes in the South, unless you thought only of the end of foreign military rule and ignored the means by which it was achieved. It did restore some kind of order, and it halted the worst kind of corruption in state government, but it took most political power from the newly enfranchised blacks (and in a few decades even that enfranchisement would be effectively eroded). And of course it did nothing to ease the race relations that had been fired to a fever pitch by the Union League and carpetbaggers and had in many places broken out into a race war whose memories would last for generations.

Which brings up most especially the consequence of abolition and Reconstruction for the black population in general. One interesting way to look at it is in terms of the basic sickness, disease, and death dealt to blacks in this period, a subject explored as best as possible by Connecticut College professor James Downs. He shows that set adrift by emancipation, with few means of surviving the collapsed plantation economy, the freedmen were victims of an "explosive epidemic outbreaks" of a whole range of diseases from yellow fever and smallpox to cholera and dysentery and died by the "tens of thousands" — which, fuzzy as it is, as he tells the story seems a decided underestimate. The failure of the Federal government, and the Reconstruction state governments as well, to create a free labor economy or in any way provide blacks with an adequate means of subsistence, meant that ex-slaves were generally unemployed or poorly paid as sharecroppers on the devastated plantations, thus making them highly susceptible to starvation and disease and causing "high mortality rates and epidemic outbreaks." The Freedmen's Bureau, to its credit, realized how serious the crisis was and attempted to do something by establishing hospitals, but by the time of its demise in 1869 it had created only 40 hospitals with a little more than 100 doctors for the black population of 3.5 million.

The failure of medical care was in essence the story with the rest of life for the freedmen: no one had planned for their future after emancipation and no one in charge much cared about it, and as soon as their problems became intractable the North washed its hands of the whole morass. It is instructive here to remember what Lincoln himself said of the freedmen's future, in a conversation with Confederate Vice President Alexander Stephens in February 1865, when the South was trying to negotiate a peaceful end to the war. Asked about what the North was prepared to do for the blacks it had emancipated, he told a story, according to Stephens, of an old farmer who was advised that a hard winter was coming up and he had to look out for his pigs; the farmer, quoting a song then popular, said "Root, hog, or die." The Freedmen's Bureau represented rather more than that sort of dismissal, but its resources were scarcely up to the job that needed to be done to give 3.5 million freedmen medical care, education, land, jobs, security, and integration into a workable economy, and one senses that behind it in Washington was an attitude not far removed from that of the old farmer.

As to education, by 1876 there were state-run public schools for blacks throughout the South, but they were poorly funded, segregated, and quite inferior. States had to pay to build and staff the schools out of deficient coffers (though indeed they devoted more of their resources in proportion to their wealth than the Northern states), and the Northern Republicans had not yet decided that Federal funding and control of education, and the minds of children black and white, were essential to the exercise of national power, though until 1870 the Freedmen's Bureau did confiscate land, buildings, books, and furniture to set up schools. The teachers as a rule were more dedicated than capable, half of them from the South, a third blacks from North and South, the rest whites from the North, most of them paid, and none too handsomely, by some 50 Northern aid and missionary societies; and there were only some 11,000 teachers in all, for a school-age population of perhaps 1.2 million, which works out to be one per a hundred-plus children. Though some 1,000 schools were established by 1870, their educational quality was indifferent at best (though they did increase literacy considerably) and after 1877 most of them no longer continued to have Northern funds or teachers.

And that, meager as it was, was considered one of the North's positive accomplishments — which, at least in comparison to land distribution and job creation, perhaps it was. The Freedmen's Bureau did indeed try to confiscate land from white plantations for the freed blacks, and in several places it was fairly successful, with perhaps 10,000 families settling on property before 1865, but in that year Johnson offered amnesty to Confederate soldiers and a return of plantation land that had been confiscated. The promise of 40 acres and a mule, often touted by the Union Leaguers and other carpetbaggers, never was met, thwarting the chances of the freedmen to economic livelihood and security, in effect condemning the black population to perpetual poverty.

As to jobs, training, and economic integration, none of that happened either. The Freedmen's Bureau initially made gestures in this direction, but it had little idea how to accomplish it, and the Radical Republicans refused to provide the significant funds that would have been needed; and of course the white population, especially the poorer whites (and some previously free blacks) who would face competition if blacks were to enter the job market, was dead set against it. As a result the largest part of the black population was condemned to tenancy and sharecropping on the land of the former plantations, only a few working for wages at jobs that they had done as slaves before, a condition that would in fact last for the better part of the next century in circumstances that were not that far removed from slavery itself.

So it is difficult to feel that the North, in sum, lived up to the "sacred obligation" that the Reverend Dabney felt it was charged with, providing greater prosperity for the freed slaves than the South had and making sure that they were not condemned to "destitution, degradation, immorality." One might want to say that freedom was worth it, no matter what the price. Yet it seems clear that it could have been achieved without such a terrible cost—as it had been everywhere else in the Western Hemisphere—if any true regard for the fate of black people had existed within Northern institutions, if Republicans had ever committed themselves to the kind of restoration that Dabney had charged them with.

In the election of 1876, Democrat Samuel Tilden won both the popular and the electoral vote over Republican Rutherford B. Hayes, with the 20 electoral votes of Florida, Louisiana, and South Carolina in dispute, since both parties declared victories in those states, the last ones still occupied by Union troops. The Republicans, desperate to stay in power after 12 years of having their way, agreed in some backroom deals with the Democrats in early 1877 that the 20 electoral votes would be given to Hayes, in return for which they would withdraw the troops from the contested states and put an official end to Reconstruction. Grant ordered the removal of the troops from Florida, a few days later the newly inaugurated Hayes ordered them removed from Louisiana and South Carolina, and as soon as they departed the Republican governments went with them and the Democrats took control in those three states. Thus the end of Reconstruction inaugurated the Democratic "Solid South" that would remain intact for nearly a century more.

IV. Afterwards

O N APRIL 16, 1888, BLACK LEADER Frederick Douglass gave a hard-hitting speech in Washington, D.C. on the twenty-sixth anniversary of the Emancipation Proclamation. He had recently taken a trip to the South and he was appalled at the conditions he found:

> I admit that the Negro…has made little progress from barbarism to civilization, and that he is in deplorable condition since his emancipation. That he is worse off, in many respects, than when he was a slave, I am compelled to admit it, but I contend that the fault is not his, but that of his heartless accusers…Though he is nominally free he is actually a slave.
>
> I here and now denounce his so-called emancipation as a stupendous fraud — a fraud upon him, a fraud upon the world.

He went on to denounce the Southern governments for failing to secure the rights and freedoms blacks rightfully and lawfully deserved, but then placed the principal part of the blame on Washington: "Take his [the black person's] relation to the national government and we shall find him a deserted, a defrauded, a swindled, and an outcast man — in law free, in fact a slave."

There was none to dispute him. So much for the Emancipation Proclamation.

Seventy-five years after this denunciation another assessment of black progress was offered, this time an even hundred years after the Proclamation, on the steps of the Lincoln memorial, by the leading black activist of his day, Martin Luther King, Jr.:

> Five score years ago, a great American, in whose symbolic shadow we stand today, signed the Emancipation Proclamation. This momentous decree came as a great beacon light of hope to millions of Negro slaves who had been seared in the flames of withering injustice. It came as a joyous daybreak to end the long night of their captivity. But one hundred years later, we must face the tragic fact that the Negro is still not free.
>
> One hundred years later, the life of the Negro is still sadly crippled by the manacles of segregation and the chains of discrimination. One hundred years later, the Negro lives on a lonely island of poverty in the midst of a vast ocean of material prosperity. One hundred years later, the Negro is still languished in the corners of American society and finds himself an exile in his own land.

There was none to dispute him, either.

It is not necessary to labor through the details of that century of black-white relations in the South to know that the seeds sown by a misconceived, mishandled, and misguided emancipation policy bore bitter, bitter fruit — as how could they not?

Soon after the Democrats regained power in the statehouses of the South they passed increasingly restrictive laws over the black population, and white society found ways of eventually taking away, by subterfuge and practice as well as by legislation, most of the rights—most particularly voting (hence serving on juries and standing for office)—that had once been granted to them. Most blacks were disenfranchised by 1880s, and thereafter Southern states established poll taxes and literacy and property tests that kept almost all blacks (and many poor whites) from the voting booth.

The separation between the races was nearly absolute, except that anywhere from half to three-quarters of the blacks lived as tenants and sharecroppers on white lands, nominally independent but caught up almost everywhere in a system of scrip payment instead of cash, and this useful only at the farm-owners' company stores. This separation was mandated by laws that were eventually named after Jim Crow—a derogatory word for blacks even before the war—passed in each state and many local communities mandating segregation of the races in public schools, parks, transportation, hotels, restaurants, housing, jobs, covenants, indeed every aspect of public life—and eventually, as in laws against interracial marriage, of private. In some places like public schools facilities were nominally often expected to be "separate but equal"—a policy upheld by the Supreme Court in 1896, by a majority of six Northerners and one Southerner—but in fact spending was never equal and black schools were woefully inferior.

And disharmony between the races was magnified by the fact that the South, crippled by the war and its aftermath, was the poorest region in the nation, and would remain so, despite considerable advances in manufacturing and banking in the mid-20th century, for the next century and a half. Its agriculture, once the principal engine of the national economy, was now decimated, although it remained the dominant occupation in the South. The sharecropper/tenancy system that replaced plantation production was acutely inefficient and unproductive since it depended on the working of small plots and without much capital investment, and hampered by the incentive-stripping scrip-payment arrangement.

The economy was further depressed by consistently low prices for cotton, after the war and throughout the 19th century (15 cents a pound in 1870, 6 cents in 1900), in part because worldwide production increased, driving prices down, and in part because the South continued to depend largely on this crop even when prices were low because it did not know how, or did not dare to take a chance, to diversify. An additional effect was exhaustion of the soils by both cotton and tobacco, limiting production; although the 5.4 million bales produced in 1859 increased to 11.4 billion in 1919, the population more than doubled, from 6.3 million to 16.9 million in that time. In the 1870-1900 period 12 per cent of the nation's population was calculated as living in poverty, primarily in the agricultural economies of the South and the Plains. A map of American per capita wealth in 1872 starkly depicts the South's weakness: the North, from Maine to Iowa, is covered almost completely with counties of high wealth, while most of the South is blank, with only scattered dots in the major cities and along the Mississippi.

An effort was made to create an industrial infrastructure in the South in the 1880s and '90s, led primarily by Atlanta's Henry Grady, managing editor of the *Atlanta Constitution* and a skilled orator, who spearheaded a group of businessmen who tried to foster new factories and induce investments from the North, where the money was and where industrialism was proceeding rapidly in these years. Grady famously made the case for the necessity of industry to a Northern audience by describing the burial of a friend:

> They buried him in the midst of a marble quarry: they cut through solid marble to make his grave; and yet a little tombstone they put above him was from Vermont. They buried him in the heart of a pine forest, and yet the pine coffin was imported from Cincinnati. They buried him within touch of an iron mine, and yet the nails in his coffin and the iron in the shovel that

dug his grave were imported from Pittsburg. They buried him by the side of the best sheep-grazing country on the earth, and yet the wool in the coffin bands and the coffin bands themselves were brought from the North. The South didn't furnish a thing on earth for that funeral but the corpse and the hole in the ground.

And he wasn't exaggerating.

Some new investment did come in to the "New South" of Grady's rhetoric, and in some places textile mills to rival New England's and iron factories to rival Pittsburgh's started operating in these decades, with non-union labor working cheaply because other economic opportunities were so slim. But Northern interests saw to it that rail rates were rigged so that these manufacturers could not undersell Northern production, so this was confined mostly to pockets like Birmingham, Atlanta, Baton Rouge, and Houston, and was never so developed that it was a significant force throughout the South — that would have to wait another hundred years.

Naturally, there were significant migrations, by both blacks and whites, out of the South, often to the west in the 19th century and then to the industrial North in the 20th. In the first wave, 1880-1900, some 140,000 blacks and 1 million whites left the South, often to Kansas and many to booming California, many others to take jobs in the industrial sectors around Pittsburgh, Chicago, and New York. A second wave, roughly 1910-1940, saw some 4 million blacks and about the same number of whites leaving the South, and though blacks suffered much of the same discrimination in the North that they had back home — in housing, schools, and hotels in particular — there were at least enough low-level jobs to provide employment for most.

The question that needs to be asked, and seldom is however, is: could it be said that the condition of the black population in the South was better in, say 1900, than it had been in 1865? They were nominally free, of course, but what Frederick Douglass had said about their economic condition amounting to continued slavery continued to be true. They were still denied the vote, they still lived largely within a white-run economy, and they still mostly worked for whites. They could own property, though much was eventually confiscated for failure to pay taxes and debts to sharecropping farmers, they often had local schools (and a few black colleges), though of lesser quality, and everywhere they had their own churches.

But in terms of family stability, health, poverty, life expectancy, and infant mortality it must be said that they were decidedly worse off.

Ask that question a hundred years later, though, and the answer is far different. The black population as a whole, at 36 million and 12 per cent of the nation, was not at the same level as the white by most measures, but it had made enormous strides in economic development, political power, social equality, education, athletics, entertainment, and American culture overall, and almost all the outward trappings of discrimination and racism had disappeared. Much of the progress began in the 1940s, when mechanized cotton-picking pushed millions of blacks north to the booming wartime factories and many into the military, after which second-class citizenship became harder to defend and in fact the U.S. Army was integrated in 1948. Pressure for equal recognition built in the 1950s, capped by the Supreme Court ordering school integration in 1954 and the subsequent court decisions enforcing it at the local level, though it took the Army in the South to effect it over considerable white resistance. In the 1960s the Civil Rights Act of 1964 and the Voting Rights Act a year later established full de jure equality, thanks to what might be called the Second Reconstruction, which, like the first, depended on Federal military might and Federal laws imposed upon the South, under which blacks gained political and legal clout that opened up mayoralties, state legislatures, and Federal offices (ultimately the Presidency) to them, and Federal courts were maneuvered to make sure that voting rights were not diminished by either de facto or de jure imposed limitations.

Although after white resistance and "white flight" in many places gradually reordered the population nationwide, particularly in the South (where in fact alone were a majority of whites in integrated schools), de facto segregation remained, especially in housing and therefore in schools, above all in urban areas. As a result, black schools everywhere have usually remained inferior and hence black entry into the middle class has remained sporadic and geographically uneven. Nationwide, black family median income, though it has hit $33,000 in recent years, remains well behind white median income at $53,000; more than half of black families earn $50,000 or more, but approximately a quarter of them are regularly below the poverty line and the black poverty rate is three times that of whites; approximately half own their own homes, even after the housing bubble burst. All in all, progress, but not yet equality.

And that is chiefly why the South, where the majority of the black population lives (55 per cent in 2010) is still relatively poorer. There has been much economic growth, without question, though textiles and steel have mostly given way to automobile plants and military bases, but it remains, over 150 years after it had been the richest region in the country, the poorest: the scars of deconstruction do not easily heal. Every state except Florida and Virginia has a higher poverty rate than the national average, and Alabama, Arkansas, Mississippi, and South Carolina regularly finish at the bottom in a variety of economic indices.

One final dark legacy of Reconstruction on present-day blacks is important to note, since it is a significant contributor to their secondary economic position and to ongoing discrimination against some portion of them: their high rates of crime and incarceration. The failure to integrate black freedmen into the economy of the post-war

South meant that most black families were condemned to poverty for many decades, inevitably leading in some places to criminal relief; add to this the deep prejudice of the white establishment and the result is certain to be high rates of incarceration, justified and other, and high rates of killing (judicial and otherwise), including some 3,400 lynchings between 1882 and 1910. Rates of black imprisonment leveled off around 1900, but increased gradually as the century went on, until by about 1970 and a Federal arbitrary and reckless "war on drugs" created a spike in numbers until by 2010 there were 2.3 million blacks (mostly men) in U.S. prisons and jails, 37 per cent of the total prison population. It has been suggested that this incarceration rate was the systematic reaction of still-racist governments, national and state, to the rise of the civil rights movement of the 1960s, but whether deliberate or not, the social and economic effect on black communities (and black families without fathers) has been serious and destructive, hampering efforts to achieve equality.

Emancipation was certainly a "stupendous fraud," but alas it was more than that. It created and nourished roots of segregation and discrimination, not in the South alone, that are so deep and noxious that a century-and-a-half later they have not been totally eradicated, even if they have in most places been ameliorated. It destroyed the economy of the South so completely, without even compensation for the most thoroughgoing seizure of private property in history, that it brought the inevitable deprivation of both black and white and the removal of any chances of black-white reconciliation for more than a century. And it condemned the black population to misery and the white to bitter racism that allowed no chance of parity, justice, rapprochement, progress, or prosperity, imprinting a sad and sorrowful legacy upon the South.

Abraham Lincoln has a lot to answer for.

BIBLIOGRAPHY

Bennett, Lerone Jr. *Forced Into Glory: Abraham Lincoln's White Dream*, Johnson Publishing, 1999, 2007.

Bensel, Richard Franklin. *Yankee Leviathan: Origins of Central State Authority in America, 1859-1877*, Cambridge University Press, 1991.

Bowers, Claude. *The Tragic Error: The Revolution After Lincoln*, Simon Press, 2007, originally 1927.

Buchanan, Patrick J. "Mr. Lincoln's War: An Irrepressible Conflict?" *Chronicles*, February 12, 2009.

Butchert, Ronald. *Schooling the Freed People: Teaching, Learning, and the Struggles for Black Freedom*, University of North Carolina Press, 2011.

Carnahan, Burrus M. *Act of Justice: Lincoln's Emancipation Proclamation and the Law of War*, University of Kentucky Press, 2007.

Chodes, John. *Destroying the Republic: Jabez Curry and the Re-education of the Old South*, Algora, 2005.

_____."The Union League," *Virginia Heritage Foundation Paper*, 1999.

Conner, Frank. *The South Under Siege, 1830-2000: A History of the Relations Between North and South*, Collards, 2002.

Coulter, E. Merton. *The South During Reconstruction, 1865-1877*, Louisiana State University Press, 1986.

Dabney, Robert Lewis. *Letter to Major General Oliver O. Howard*, (http://americascaesar.com/etext/dabney_letter_howard.htm)

Downs, James. *Sick from Freedom: African-American Illness and Suffering during the Civil War and Reconstruction*, Oxford University Press, 2012.

Douglass, Frederick. "I Denounce the So-Called Emancipation," (http://historyisaweapon.com/defcon1/douglassfraud.html)

DiLorenzo, Thomas J. *The Real Lincoln: A New Look at Abraham Lincoln, His Agenda, and an Unnecessary War*, Three Rivers Press, 2002, 2003.

Edgar, Walter. *South Carolina: A History*, University of South Carolina Press, 1998.

Elkins, Stanley M. *Slavery: A Problem in American Institutional & Intellectual Life*, Grosset & Dunlap, 1963.

Emison, John Avery. *Lincoln Uber Alles: Dictatorship Comes to America*, Pelican, 2009.

Faust, Drew Gilpin. *This Republic of Suffering*, Knopf, 2008.

Fogel, Robert William, and Engerman, Stanley L. *Time on the Cross: The Economics of American Negro Slavery*, Norton, 1974, 1989.

Foner, Eric. *The Fiery Trial: Abraham Lincoln and American*

Slavery, Norton, 2010.

_____. *Reconstruction: America's Unfinished Revolution, 1863-1877*, Harper, 2002.

Franklin, John Hope. *The Emancipation Proclamation*, Doubleday, 1963, 1995.

Genovese, Eugene. *The Slaveholders' Dilemma*, University of South Carolina Press, 1992.

Goldfield, David. *America Aflame: How the Civil War Created a Nation*, Bloomsbury, 2011.

Goodwin, Doris Kearns. *Team of Rivals*, Simon & Schuster, 2005.

Graham, John Remington. *Blood Money: The Civil War and the Federal Reserve*, Pelican, 2006.

Guelzo, Allen C. *Lincoln's Emancipation Proclamation: The End of Slavery In America*, Simon & Schuster, 2004.

Guterl, Matthew Pratt. *American Mediterranean: Southern Slaveholders in the Age of Emancipation*, Harvard University Press, 2008.

Hacker, J. David. "A Census-Based Count of the Civil War Dead," *Civil War History*, Vol. 57, No. 4, December 2011.

Holzer, Harold, Medford, Edna Greene, and Williams, Frank J. *The Emancipation Proclamation*, Louisiana State University, 2006.

Hummel, Jeffrey Rogers. *Emancipating Slaves, Enslaving Free Men: A History of the American Civil War*, Open Court, 1996.

Kennedy, James Ronald and Walter Donald. *The South Was Right!* Pelican, 1991,1994.

Lemann, Nicholas. *The Promised Land: The Great Black Migration and How It Changed America*, Knopf, 1991.

Levine, Bruce. *Confederate Emancipation: Southern Plans to Free and Arm Slaves During the Civil War*, Oxford University Press, 2006.

Livingston, Donald W. *Why the War Was Not About Slavery*, SCV Sesquicentennial Series, 2010.

_____."The Moral Accounting of the Union and the Confederacy," *Journal of Libertarian Studies*, Vol. 16. No. 2, Spring 2002.

Masters, Edgar Lee. *Lincoln: The Man*, Foundation for American Education, 1997, originally Dodd, Mead, 1931.

Magness, Philip W. and Page, Sebastian N. *Colonization After Emancipation*, University of Missouri, 2011.

Martinez, J. Michael. *Coming for to Carry Me Home: Race in America from Abolitionism to Jim Crow*, Rowman & Littlefield, 2012.

McClelland, P.D., and Zeckhauser, R. J. *Demographic Dimensions of the New Republic, 1800-60*, Cambridge University Press, 1982, 2002.

Moore, Wilbert E. *American Negro Slavery and Abolition: A Sociological Study*, The Third Press, 1971.

Neeley, Mark E. Jr. "The Lincoln Administration and Arbitrary Arrests," *Journal of Abraham Lincoln Association*, Vol. 5, # 1, 1983.

Paulino, Ernest N. *Foundation of the American Empire*, Cornell University, 1973.

Powell, Jim. *Greatest Emancipation*, Palgrave Macmillan, 2008.

Stokes, Karen. *South Carolina Civilians in Sherman's Path: Stories of Courage Amid Civil War Destruction*, History Press, 2012.

Stromberg, Joseph. "A Plain Folk Perspective on Reconstruction," *Journal of Libertarian Studies*, Vol. 16, No. 2, Spring 2002.

Summerville, Diane Miller. "Will They Ever Be Able to Forget":

Confederate Soldiers and Mental Illness in the Defeated South," in *Weirding the War: Stories from the Civil War's Ragged Edges*, ed. Stephen Berry, University of Georgia Press, 2011.

_____. quoted in *Charleston Post & Courier*, May 31, 2012

Warren, Robert Penn. *The Legacy of the Civil War*, Bison Books, 1998 (originally 1961).

Wesley, Charles. "Negroes as Soldiers in the Confederate Army," *Journal of Negro History*, Vol. 4, No. 3, 1919.

White, Howard Ray. *Abe Lincoln's First Shot Strategy*, Self, 2011.

Wilson, Clyde N. *Defending Dixie: Essays in Southern History and Culture*, Foundation for American Education, 2005.

EMANCIPATION PROCLAMATION

January 1, 1863

By the President of the United States of America: A Proclamation.

Whereas, on the twenty-second day of September, in the year of our Lord one thousand eight hundred and sixty-two, a proclamation was issued by the President of the United States, containing, among other things, the following, to wit:

"That on the first day of January, in the year of our Lord one thousand eight hundred and sixty-three, all persons held as slaves within any State or designated part of a State, the people whereof shall then be in rebellion against the United States, shall be then, thenceforward, and forever free; and the Executive Government of the United States, including the military and naval authority thereof, will recognize and maintain the freedom of such persons, and will do no act or acts to repress such persons, or any of them, in any efforts they may make for their actual freedom.

"That the Executive will, on the first day of January aforesaid, by proclamation, designate the States and parts of States, if any, in which the people thereof, respectively, shall then be in rebellion against the United States; and the fact that any State, or the people thereof, shall on that day be, in good faith, represented in the Congress of the United States by members chosen thereto at elections wherein a majority of the qualified voters of such State shall have participated, shall, in the absence of strong countervailing testimony, be deemed conclusive evidence that such State, and the people thereof, are not then in rebellion against the United States."

Now, therefore I, Abraham Lincoln, President of the United States, by virtue of the power in me vested as Commander-in-Chief, of the Army and Navy of the United States in time of actual armed rebellion against the authority and government of the United States, and as a fit and necessary war measure for suppressing said rebellion, do, on this first day of January, in the year of our Lord one thousand eight hundred and sixty-three, and in accordance with my purpose so to do publicly proclaimed for the full period of one hundred days, from the day first above mentioned, order and designate as the States and parts of States wherein the people thereof respectively, are this day in rebellion against the United States, the following, to wit:

Arkansas, Texas, Louisiana, (except the Parishes of St. Bernard, Plaquemines, Jefferson, St. John, St. Charles, St. James Ascension, Assumption, Terrebonne, Lafourche, St. Mary, St. Martin, and Orleans, including the City of New Orleans) Mississippi, Alabama, Florida, Georgia, South Carolina, North Carolina, and Virginia, (except the forty-eight counties designated as West Virginia, and also the counties of Berkley, Accomac, Northampton, Elizabeth City, York, Princess Ann, and Norfolk, including the cities of Norfolk and Portsmouth[)], and which excepted parts, are for the present, left precisely as if this proclamation were not issued.

And by virtue of the power, and for the purpose aforesaid, I do order and declare that all persons held as slaves within said designated States, and parts of States, are, and henceforward shall be free; and that the Executive government of the United States, including the military and naval authorities thereof, will recognize and maintain the freedom of said persons.

And I hereby enjoin upon the people so declared to be free to abstain from all violence, unless in necessary self-defence; and I recommend to them that, in all cases when allowed, they labor faithfully for reasonable wages.

And I further declare and make known, that such persons of suitable condition, will be received into the armed service of the United States to garrison forts, positions, stations, and other places, and to man vessels of all sorts in said service.

And upon this act, sincerely believed to be an act of justice, warranted by the Constitution, upon military necessity, I invoke the considerate judgment of mankind, and the gracious favor of Almighty God.

In witness whereof, I have hereunto set my hand and caused the seal of the United States to be affixed.

Done at the City of Washington, this first day of January, in the year of our Lord one thousand eight hundred and sixty three, and of the Independence of the United States of America the eighty-seventh.

By the President: ABRAHAM LINCOLN

WILLIAM H. SEWARD, Secretary

ABOUT THE AUTHOR

KIRKPATRICK SALE is the author of a dozen iconoclastic books, including the devolutionist, small-government classic *Human Scale*. A prolific and highly independent scholar and journalist, he has published hundreds of articles. In keeping with his devolutionist perspective, Sale has been a leader of the Second Vermont Republic and the director of the Middlebury Institute. He has been called "the father of modern secessionist movements." Since moving from New England to Mount Pleasant, South Carolina, he has been a delegate to the Southern National Congress

ALSO BY KIRKPATRICK SALE

The Land and People of Ghana, Lippincott, 1963, 1972.

SDS: The rise and development of the Students for a Democratic Society, Random House, 1973. Vintage Books edition (paperback) 1974.

Power Shift: The Rise of the Southern Rim and Its Challenge to the Eastern Establishment. New York: Random House, 1975.

Human Scale. New York: Coward, McCann & Geoghegan, 1980.

Dwellers in the Land: The Bioregional Vision. San Francisco: Sierra Club Books, 1985.

The Conquest of Paradise: Christopher Columbus and the Columbian Legacy, Knopf, 1990.

Rebels Against the Future: The Luddites and Their War on the Industrial Revolution: Lessons for the Computer Age, Addison Wesley, 1995.

The Green Revolution: The American Environmental Movement, 1962, 1992, Hill and Wang, 1993.

Why the Sea Is Salt: Poems of Love and Loss, iUniverse, 2001.

The Fire of His Genius: Robert Fulton and the American Dream, Free Press, 2001.

After Eden: The Evolution of Human Domination, Duke University Press, 2006.

FOREWORD - INTRODUCTIONS

Kohr, Leopold. *Breakdown of Nations*, E.P. Dutton, 1978.

Schumacher, E. E. *Small Is Beautiful*, Harper Perennial, 1989.

Lanz, Tobias. *Beyond Capitalism and Socialism*, HIS Press, 2008.

Naylor, Thomas. *Secession*, Feral House, 2008.

AVAILABLE FROM
SHOTWELL PUBLISHING

Southern Independence. Why War? - The War to Prevent Southern Independence (2015) By Dr. Charles T. Pace with Foreword by Dr. Clyde N. Wilson

The "American Civil War" was not a "Civil War" and everyone knows it, yet the use of this misleading and inaccurate designation is almost universal in the English speaking world.

Dr. Charles T. Pace has been the first to use a precisely accurate term for the U.S. "Civil War" — the WAR TO PREVENT SOUTHERN INDEPENDENCE. In this work he traces how what he calls the Northern Money Party preferred war to allowing the South to get free of its economic domination. He reveals aspects of Abraham Lincoln's life and actions that even Professor Thomas DiLorenzo missed.

Along the way, reflecting on his long career as a family physician in North Carolina, the author describes what was good in a Southern life shared by blacks and whites over many generations.

FOR A COMPLETE LISTING OF CURRENT AND FORTHCOMING TITLES,

PLEASE VISIT

WWW.SHOTWELLPUBLISHING.COM

Made in the USA
Las Vegas, NV
02 April 2024